Bugging In or Bugging Out?

I0428561

By Robert Paine

© 2014

When disaster strikes, are you going to hunker down or hit the road?

In this book you will learn:
- The main differences between Bugging In and Bugging Out
- How to pack a Bug Out Bag for each member of your family, without going overboard.
- How to fortify your home and yourself for ultimate safety and protection.
- Tips and Tricks for deciding which method is right for you
- And much, much more!

Sign up for Robert's Mailing List to be notified of **New Releases** and **Special Sales**: http://eepurl.com/zvm11

Other Books by Robert Paine:

Bugging Out or Bugging In?

Introduction

There are plenty of guides that tell you all about bugging out and what to do if you need to bug in, but this guide will cover each option in depth. You will find checklists of items you will want to get together to make bugging in or bugging out work for you and your family. There are plenty of tips, tricks and best practices to help you be successful in your goal to be prepared for nearly anything. You will find everything you ever needed to know about storing food, water and other necessary supplies.

This is the kind of guide you will reference often as you pack your bug out bag and stockpile food and water. There are so many factors to consider when it comes to prepping it is easy to overlook a small, but very important detail. This book is meant to guide you through every aspect of prepping while providing you with ideas and options you can apply to your life and where you live.

What is Bugging?

If you have an interest in survival and prepping, you have probably heard the term "bugging out" or "bugging in" quite a bit. It is essentially what prepping is all about. So, what is it? The term bugging was originally used by military personnel. When things became too dangerous for troops and other military personnel to remain in a location, they would bug out. Meaning, they got out of an area before there was an invasion or attack. Now, if you want to get really technical, the phrase is rumored to have stemmed from actual bugs scattering from a location, but that cannot possibly be proven. Another theory is the British military used the term buggered out and the Americans quickly picked up on it. From there, civilians have begun using the term in prepping circles.

Bugging is the act of surviving the aftermath of an event that leaves the world as you know it upside down and inside out. If you have read blogs or other eBooks about survival and prepping, you have probably seen the terms, TEOTWAWKI and SHTF. The first stands for The End Of The World As We Know It and that last is a little more vulgar and stands for when S*** Hits The Fan. When one or both of these things happen, your bugging plan goes into motion.

If you haven't taken the time to prepare, the hours and days following a major event can be overwhelming. It can be extremely devastating to your state of mind, which survivalists will tell you is a huge concern. Your mind is a powerful tool. Imagine the comfort you will feel knowing you have food, water and medical supplies when the rest of your neighborhood has been turned upside down. Although you will still have a lot on your plate, marking off the necessities of life can make a dire situation, tolerable.

People who have taken the time to learn about what is needed to survive an event are referred to as preppers. Prepping to live seems pretty natural, but many are still not on board. When you add the word bugging to the equation, people really get uncomfortable. However, for those who understand what it means, it is actually a little comforting knowing you are prepared to bug in or bug out.

What's the Difference Between Bugging In or Bugging Out

You understand the idea of "bugging," but how do you know when it is time to leave the comfort and safety of your home or other location and head out for the open wilderness, forest or whatever the surroundings? Bugging out is setting out with whatever you can carry on your back or in some cases, in your car. This is always going to be a decision that needs to be made hours or days before an impending event. If you feel like your location is secure enough for you to bug in, that will be the focus of your preps.

City dwellers and those that live in the suburbs often plan to bug out to a secret location where they will bug in for the duration. Bugging out involves carrying a single or several bags that have been packed ahead of time. The bags are filled with the necessities you need to survive in the outdoors.

If you know your home is not a suitable place to try and ride out a major storm, a terrorist attack or other catastrophic event, you need to make plans to bug out. The moment you see a major storm headed your way or the moment you know an attack is imminent, it is time to bug out if the safety of your home will be compromised. Now, depending on the scenario, you may only need to bug out to a hotel or a relative's home in a neighboring city or town. It is impossible to predict with accuracy what kind of situation you will be faced with.

On the flip side of that, if things are going downhill in a hurry, you need to do what is necessary to secure your home to bug in. If it isn't safe to leave or you don't think you can make it to another location without encountering danger, bugging in is usually the best bet. When you are in your own home, you have those creature comforts you have come to love and appreciate.

Every family will have to make the decision based on the circumstances. Later in the book, we will discuss the things that you need to do to prepare for either scenario. Every prepper knows you have to be ready to deal with almost anything. Putting all your "eggs" in the bugging in basket could be extremely dangerous. You just never know when an attack is going to hit your home. You also don't know if you will be able to safely bug out when the time comes. You need your home to be stocked enough to keep you and your family alive until it is safe to bug out.

The old saying, "The best laid plans of mice and men often go awry," can and should be applied to prepping. You just never know.

Common Reasons for Prepping

In the survival world, you will find a wide number of reasons given for why people are getting involved in the prepping movement. You could ask 20 different preppers the same question and you are likely to get 20 different answers. The reasons people decide to start prepping vary widely, but the goal is always the same—to survive a catastrophic event.

The following are just a few of the reasons people choose to prep.

- War on our soil
- Civil unrest
- Terrorist attack
- Natural disaster i.e. hurricanes, earthquakes, severe storm
- EMP—electromagnetic pulse from the sun
- Pandemic
- Worldwide economic collapse
- Personal comfort in case of job loss, family tragedy
- Religious reasons
- Major climate change

Your reasons may be all of the above or something totally different. Ultimately, if you are prepping for a specific event, like a pandemic, your preps may be a little different than somebody who is prepping for a major financial collapse. No matter your reason for prepping, it is always done with the same goal of surviving. Parents tend to make up a majority of the prepping population. It is instinct to want to protect your children and that includes helping them survive situations that could otherwise be life-threatening.

Preppers have taken the initiative to prepare for a disaster because it is highly likely there will not be help readily available in the aftermath. When there is some catastrophic event, it could take weeks or even months before there is any relief. You have to be able to survive on your own without the luxury of having a store to run to or the ability to call 911 or receive government assistance. Many people do not fully understand what it is like to truly be on their own. We have become so accustomed to getting everything we need at a store or calling for help, it will be a major adjustment for everybody. Those who have prepared will even struggle a bit to come to terms with the situation. People who didn't prepare are going to be devastated.

They are going to be forced to do things they may have never considered in the past just to survive. That does not bode well for society. Crime will likely be out of control as people become savage in their search for food, water and critical medicines. With no law to regulate those who are killing and thieving, it will be a very rough world.

Although preppers tend to be a quiet bunch who don't like to talk a lot about what they have (for good reason), you will find there are plenty who would prefer it if the entire population did their own prepping. It would make things much more civilized if everybody had their own food stores to turn to. Unfortunately, that isn't the case and the majority of the population will scoff at the idea of stocking up on food and water.

Bugging Out

Bugging out is something that requires careful consideration. If you are leaving the safety and comfort of your home and heading off into the forest, desert or whatever the terrain, you cannot afford to forget a single item. One single tool could mean the difference between life and death. If bugging out is your plan when things go sideways, it is important to make sure the whole family is prepared to survive without the comforts of the home. You would be doing yourself a major disservice if you were to haphazardly run through the home tossing things in a bag that you think will help you survive in the minutes before or after a disaster. It would likely send you off into the wild blue yonder with a false sense of security. When it came time to set up a shelter or procure water, the large amount of food and your toothbrush are not going to help you.

It takes a great deal of planning to pick and choose the right items to put in the bug out bag. You should also spend some time packing the bag carefully. The more organized your packing job, the more stuff you will be able to fit in. When you are forced to act in haste, your decision-making suffers.

What is a Bug Out Bag

In order to bug out, you need a bug out bag. This is the bag that is going to keep you alive. In a serious catastrophe, everything you own in life could very well be in that bag. Without stores or somewhere to buy supplies, what you pack in your bug out bag will be all that you have to carry you through a disaster.

A bug out bag is a backpack filled with key tools that will aid in survival. The bag is going to hold your food, water and various tools needed to get more food, clean water and build a shelter. The bags are packed and ready to grab when it is time to bug out. When you have a bug out bag, you don't have to spend precious minutes deciding what to pack and shove it into a bag haphazardly. If you go this route, you can pretty much guarantee you are going to forget something important.

Every prepper and survival expert knows the key to staying alive and making it through a disaster situation is a well-stocked bug out bag. Our military carries backpacks into the field in case they are not able to make it back to camp. These bags are essentially their survival packs. A bug out bag is basically the same thing, but used by civilians. Our military has come up with some pretty awesome ideas and preppers are constantly integrating them into their own lifestyles and preps. With all the experience and hands on training in the military, it is safe to say what works for them will work for civilians. There is no need to try and reinvent the wheel so to speak. Learn from them and you will save yourself a lot of time and energy.

Picking the Right Bag

Bigger packs are not always better. Take some time picking out a backpack that you can wear comfortably. Ideally, framed packs are your best bet. You have the option of choosing from an internal frame or an external frame. In many ways, they are equal. However, external frames tend to be a bit heavier. There is some new technology that has made external frame packs a little lighter, but unless you are willing to spend a great deal of money on one of these packs, your best bet is an internal frame.

Framed backpacks are ideal because they spread the weight of the pack across your hips and take some of the pressure off your back and shoulders. You can also get a lot more supplies in a framed pack. The downside to the framed packs is their cost. They can be very expensive, upwards of $300 for a good, sturdy pack. You can often find the packs at secondhand stores and online. However, you want to inspect the pack carefully to ensure the stitching is still tight and your goods are not going to fall out as you climb a hill.

If you are opting to go with a standard backpack, make sure it has adequate shoulder padding, lots of pockets inside and out to maximize space and is not made of a material that is prone to shredding. Wide straps are ideal. When the backpack is loaded down, you don't want thin straps that will dig into your shoulders as you walk. A hip belt is a very important accessory. It will keep the pack positioned on your back so it isn't flopping around when you are walking and climbing. You need to be able to maintain your balance and a shifting backpack will impede your ability to move. A sternum clip is nice, but not necessarily a necessity. It further anchors the pack to your body by maximizing the chest bone.

Yet another concern is the material that will be against your back. You will want to choose a bag that has a mesh or breathable lining that will be against your body. While it will still be hot and you will likely still sweat a little where the pack rests against your body, you don't want it to be overly hot. This will create chafing and be uncomfortable in general. The breathable material will allow for some airflow to reduce the majority of the sweating.

You also should avoid brightly colored packs. If you are bugging out, chances are you don't want to stand out like a sore thumb. You want to be able to blend into your surroundings. Higher quality packs are worth the extra cost. A flimsy bag will not be able to withstand a lot of wear and tear. You need something that is rugged and durable. Because the bag is going to hold your life in it, it is a wise decision to make the investment to buy at least one really good bag. You can buy a few other bags that are of a lesser quality to keep on hand for family members to pack out.

Pick a bag that has lots of loops, straps and zippered pockets that allow you to hang things from the outside of your bag. Outside, zippered pockets are ideal. These allow you to store things that you need quickly and most often, like flashlights, water purification methods and a knife. Zippers keep gear where it is supposed to be. Invest in what the military refers to as MOLLE clips. These are clips that you hang from the outside of your pack and are used to hold gear you need in a hurry. The clips detach from the bag with a simple snap, which allows you to reach critical gear quickly without digging through your bag or unzipping pockets. Your whistle is best left hanging from your bag as is a flashlight or canteen.

Newer bags that have been designed for hikers have camelbacks integrated into the pack. These are luxurious! You can carry water without packing around a heavy bottle. A camelback is a flat bladder that would sit across your back. A straw is connected and brought over your shoulder for you to sip on when you get thirsty. These are ingenious and oh so valuable in a bug out situation.

Size matters when choosing a bag for each member of the family. REI has created a chart for you to use to help you determine what size of bag will fit best on your body. The length of your torso will determine which pack is right for you. See below.

Pack Size	Torso Length
Extra Small	Up to 15 ½ inches
Small	16 to 17 ½ inches
Medium/Regular	18 to 19 ½ inches
Large/Tall	20+ inches

Some people will opt to use a duffel bag, but this is generally not a good idea. They are not easy to carry. While you can certainly pack a lot more gear in a duffel bag, they are just obnoxious to try and carry over rough terrain.

What to Pack in Your Bug Out Bag

This is probably the most important bag you will ever pack in your life. It requires careful consideration and planning. Unfortunately, you can't pack everything, including the kitchen sink. You are going to be carrying this bag on your back and cannot afford to pack it so full it becomes a major burden. A bag that is heavier than you can pack with ease will hinder you and can cause you to trip, fall or be unable to move as fast as you need to. There is a fine line between packing too much and packing enough to survive. Bigger packs are not always better. While some burly men are okay carrying 70 pounds on their backs, the general population is not cut out for that. As you pack your bag, you are going to want to weigh it on your bathroom scale and test it out on your own back.

The following list includes the things you absolutely must have in your pack. Another list will outline some additional items that can make life a little easier, but are not necessarily crucial to your immediate survival. Keep in mind, these supply lists are made with the idea of sustaining one to two people. If you are bugging out with your family, you will want to create bug out bags for each member. In the next section, we will discuss the process of creating a bug out bag for a child—yes, they need one!

Essential Bug Out Bag Supplies

- Water purification method; tablets, filtration straws, portable filters
- Fire starting method—at least 2 ways; waterproof matches, lighter, magnesium stick, flint rod and steel
- Cordage i.e. paracord, rope
- Canteen or collapsible water bottle
- Good quality knife
- Poncho
- Trash bags—these have numerous uses i.e. water containment, ground barrier, poncho and etc…
- 2 Mylar survival blankets—these aren't meant to keep you warm necessarily, but make an excellent heat shield and can keep you dry. Choose high quality blankets when possible.
- First aid kit—see next section for what to pack
- Folding shovel

- Headlamp—LEDs are best, lightweight and last longer than a typical flashlight
- Wool socks
- Work gloves
- Compass
- Whistle
- Energy bars
- Insect repellant
- Sunscreen
- Chapstick
- Medications you need for survival
- EpiPen if you have one

Those are the bare minimums. The next list you can pick and choose from based on your personal needs and preferences.

- Sleeping mat
- Personal hygiene i.e. toothpaste, toothbrush, soap, toilet paper
- Feminine hygiene products
- Wet napkins
- Washcloth-compact cloths that are about the size of a 50-cent piece are perfect
- Tinder bundle material
    - Lint from the dryer

- Dried moss
- Cotton balls soaked in Vaseline
- Dried grass
- Multi-tool—Swiss Army knife
- Tarp
- Wool blanket
- Change of underwear
- Freeze-dried food packs
- Portable stove—mini burners
- Metal cup
- Hand crank radio—battery powered is optional, but batteries are heavy
- Duct tape
- Self-defense i.e. gun, knife, Taser, pepper spray
- Ziploc bags for storing supplies, keeps bugs out and gear dry
- Backpack cover to keep pack dry
- Fishing line and hooks
- Super glue—serves a number of purposes and can be used to close wounds
- Sewing kit
- Bandana—used for signaling or covering the face to block dust or keep warm
- Light sticks

The following list will help you put together a first aid kit to store in your bug out bag. Keep in mind; this is meant to be a personal use kit. You can certainly give out a band-aid or two, but your supplies are going to be limited so use cautiously. You will want to store your first aid kit in a small pouch or large Ziploc bag. For small kits, pencil cases work great for keeping all of your medical supplies together. You could also use makeup bags that are clear. This makes it easy to see what you need. Hard cases tend to be heavier. Gauze will still work, even if it is a little smashed. You could ensure your first aid supplies stay dry by putting them in a small case and then putting the case in the large Ziploc bag.

- 2 2x2 gauze pads 2 4x4 gauze pads
- Medical tape
- 4 band-aids in each size, small, medium, large
- Gauze roll—remove from box and put in small sandwich bag to save space
- 4 pain reliever tablets i.e. ibuprofen/acetaminophen
- 2 packs of aspirin
- Triple antibiotic cream
- Alcohol wipes
- Mole bandages for blisters
- Butterfly stitch bandages
- ACE bandage
- Latex gloves—2 pair minimum

- Antihistamine tablets—Benadryl
- Pepto-Bismol tablets—stop diarrhea, which could lead to dehydration
- 2 absorbent compress dressings—feminine napkins work great!
- Tweezers
- Medical scissors
- Iodine
- Garlic tablets—garlic is a natural antibiotic and can help fight an infection when there are no antibiotics
- Small book that outlines basic First Aid

Do not get carried away with your first aid kit. Your bug out bag and accompanying first aid kit are meant to get you from point A to point B. The kits are not meant to be a complete kit that can be used to do surgery in the field—if you even knew how to do that. If you have a bug out location in mind, store your major medical supplies there.

A note about water filtration devices:

There are plenty of different options on the market to clean water. However, you must realize you need something that is portable and will last longer than a single use. Tablets are easy and fairly quick to use, but when they run out, what will you do? Filters are excellent as well, but again, after filtering so many gallons of water they are ineffective. Boiling is one of the only constants you have, which is why a cup or pot is important to have. You need to be able to heat your water to kill off pathogens.

When you are shopping for your water cleaning tools, there are two main kinds, filters and purifiers. They are not the same.

Filters - Filters are removing visible impurities and the majority of bacteria that may be in the water. Filters do NOT remove most viruses from the water. Filters are a physical barrier, like charcoal or a cloth that the water passes through. You need to choose a filter that filters up to .02 microns. This means the filtering system catches the tiniest germs and bacteria that may be in the water.

Purifiers - Purification is chemically treated water that effectively kills bacteria, viruses and neutralizes most chemical contaminants. However, if you know a body of water is filled with fertilizer run off, it is best to avoid it altogether. Bleach or iodine are the best ways to purify your water. Those little tablets you are packing in your emergency preps are purifiers. If you are dealing with water that has some floaties in it, run it through your bandana before dropping a tablet in.

Some people will pack along charcoal tablets to create their own filters. This will work. You could also use charred wood from a campfire or burned out tree if necessary. Charcoal grabs onto bacteria and traps it when water is run through it.

Bug Out Bags for Kids

The kids need their own bug out bags. This will help you ensure you have enough supplies for the whole family and takes advantage of every available person to help carry supplies. Everybody needs to pull their weight in a survival situation. While you don't need to load the kids up with a bag quite as big as yours, you still want to make sure it is filled with the essentials. You will also want to choose a bag that is a bit smaller and fits the child. Refer to the chart above. An overly large bag could make it difficult for a child to walk and even cause trips and falls. A fall in a survival situation is much more serious. There isn't an emergency room to run to if the child breaks an arm or splits their lip open. It can be a little difficult to find a plain child's bag in a subdued color, but look around and check the internet. You don't want your little girl carrying a bright pink Hello Kitty backpack that will stand out in a copse of trees.

The list of supplies in the first essential list can be packed into a child's backpack with room to spare. Use common sense when it comes to stocking large knives in a child's bug out bag. It isn't necessary for the child to carry a foldable shovel as well if you have one. Use your best judgment when packing bags for kids under the age of about 12. Some kids are better prepared to use the gear you are packing. If you trust your 6-year-old to carry matches, than go for it.

When you pack bug out bags for young kids, you are doing so with the intention of them being with you or another adult with an adequately stocked bug out bag. However, you also want your child to be able to survive if they get lost or have to set out on their own. This would be in extreme situations, but in the midst of a serious crisis, things do tend to be extreme. Some people distribute supplies among the family in somewhat of a divide and conquer approach. This is a great idea if the entire family is traveling together, but if one person has the fire starting material and another has the water purification tablets and the group gets separated, all of the bug out bag planning in the world isn't going to make that situation any better. Every bag should have the basic necessities. Spread out the extra, non-essential gear if you would like.

When you think about it, having all the extra gear when you do reach your destination is a boon. Instead of having a couple bags of waterproof matches, you will have close to 10 or however many you pack in each of your family member's bags.

If you have a teenager who drives or may be at work or school when things get crazy, you will want them to be able to make it to a designated location as well. You can typically count on a teenager knowing how to use a knife effectively as well as the remaining gear. Discuss each piece of gear in the bag with your teen before it is ever actually needed. Have the teen keep the bag in their car.

In many cases, your kids are not going to want to carry around two backpacks - one for school and one for their survival gear. It just won't work. Keep a bug out bag at home for your child and create a small kit they can keep in the bottom of their school backpack. Those little pencil pouches are excellent for a few key pieces of survival gear as well. Toss in a bag of water purification tablets, waterproof matches, Mylar blanket, and a multi-tool. This is best for a child that is responsible enough to leave the gear alone and not "play" with it. Those few necessities can keep them alive until you get to them or they get to you.

A well-stocked bug out bag is great, but if you have never used the gear and are not familiar with it, it will do you little good in a survival situation. Spend some time at least once a month working with the gear with the kids. Trying to start a fire in the rain isn't easy, especially when trying to use a magnesium stick. It is a skill that requires practice. You can save yourself some money by purchasing quality gear that can be used repeatedly. Training in a survival situation is not ideal and could ultimately cost lives. Take a hike or go out on a campout with the kids and practice! Teach them about the tools they have in their bags and when they would want to use each tool.

Where to Store Bug Out Bags

A bug out bag will be worth more than a truckload of gold in a serious crisis. You will want to protect it and hide it from those who will be willing to kill you to take it from you. When the world is in chaos, people do things they normally wouldn't do. Your next door neighbor may suddenly become your biggest enemy if he wants and needs what you have to help his family survive. There is no law and there will certainly be no order as your friends, neighbors and co-workers all fight to survive. Those who haven't prepared are going to be coming straight for your front door if they know with certainty you have gear that will keep them alive.

You need to stash your bug out bag in a location that is safe and secure, but easily accessible by you and your family members. Sticking it by your front door for all visitors to see is not a good idea. If you plan on guests coming over for a barbecue or to watch the game, just use common sense when it comes to leaving your gear in plain view. People get curious and they will ask questions. While you certainly want to discuss the topic of having a backup plan and what people can do to prepare, you definitely don't want to advertise what you have.

The back of a closet, behind some food in a pantry or in an old bucket in the garage are all good places to hide your bag. Some people get creative and hide their bag in crates that are masked as furniture. A wooden box makes a great place to hide a couple of bags. Cover the crate with a pretty tablecloth; add some knick knacks or a lamp and guest will never realize what they are looking at. The idea is for you to know exactly where the bags are and be able to reach them quickly. Don't get too carried away with your hiding tactics. If you have to use a hammer to pull of sheetrock or tear into a floor to get to your bag, it defeats the purpose.

It is a really good idea to have more than a single bug out bag. You never know when a disaster could destroy your home and your survival gear with it. Ideally, you will want to have a bag in your car as well. Hide it under a blanket in the backseat or in the trunk. Many cars have a small space under the floor of the trunk. This is a great place to stash a small bag. A bag in an outdoor storage shed in case your home is destroyed gives you another layer of protection. It is always better to be over prepared than under.

Check out some of the other places you can hide your bug out bags.

- In a rubber tote marked "Christmas decorations. Throw a strand of lights and garland over the top, just in case somebody looks.
- Inside a box in a closet marked, "winter clothes" or something along those lines
- At the bottom of a garbage can in the garage or on the porch. Put a liner in the can and add a few bits of trash.
- A hollowed out area under a stairwell, camouflage the area with a rug or hang a picture if it is in a wall

You will want to get creative with your own hiding spots. Just remember to keep the bug out bag somewhat accessible so you can grab it in a hurry. You will also want your family members to know where it is at and how to get to it should they be in charge of retrieving the bug out gear. There are times when you won't be home or you could be injured. There are some places you don't want to put your bug out bag. Hiding your bag in a place that can cause your gear to become damaged will defeat your purpose of survival.

- Areas that are prone to wetness i.e. under kitchen sink, on the floor in basement

- Avoid areas that are prone to extreme heat—this can degrade things like your food supplies and Mylar blanket. Ideally you want a place that has an average temperature of 80 degrees or less.
- Avoid areas that are prone to extreme cold—outdoor sheds in areas where the temperatures drop below 10 degrees is not a good idea.
- Keep the bag out of direct sunlight

Bugging In

If leaving your home is not the best plan for you and your family, you need to plan to hunker down and weather whatever catastrophe has stricken your area. This is probably the ideal thing to do for most. There are numerous benefits to staying in your own home in an area you are familiar with. Maybe you have like-minded neighbors who will be able to offer support. Small communities provide normalcy and can help make an area a bit safer.

However, if you live in the middle of a city, hunkering down after a major disaster isn't always a good idea. A heavily populated area will mean more people trying to survive on little to no supplies. Those people are going to come looking and your home may be compromised. With that said, there is a lot to be said for bugging in. It gives you the chance to create a healthy stockpile of food, water and of course, it provides you shelter. Being able to stay in your own home also provides a level of comfort and security that is vitally important in uncertain times. There are many preppers who essentially prepare for the worst—bugging out, but hope for the best—bugging in.

If you only need to ride out a storm or some similar event that will be over in a matter of days, staying home is usually the best idea. The government often advises people to do this. It is safer to stay inside, with your head down so to speak. Wait to leave the house until you hear it is safe to do so.

What to Store for Bugging In

When you think about bugging in, it can be a bit overwhelming. This section will break it down into easy to swallow bite size pieces. Keep in mind, you don't want to run out and max out your credit card trying to buy everything you need to keep your family alive for a year. Be frugal and buy food items when they are on sale. Do some shopping around to compare prices. Buying online is usually going to be your best bet, but there are often closeout sales in local business that can save you money on shipping.

You need to assume you are going to be living in your home without access to outside food, water and other supplies. What you have in your home when disaster strikes is what you will have to live on. There are a lot of different considerations you will have to think about when planning to bug in. You have to plan on taking care of your entire family for days or even months. Be prepared to do a little math as you determine how much food and water you need to store. If you are new to the idea of prepping, it is helpful to start small. Begin with stores to last 30 days. Once you have that, build up to 3 months and then 6 months and finally, a year's worth of food. In a way, you can think of it as preparing to run a marathon. You need to do some training first before you jump in with both feet.

Food

Your food storage should be enough to last at the bare minimum 3 days. That is the very lowest you should ever have on hand at any given time. Ideally, you should stock enough food to feed your family for about 30 days. Available space, funds and your personal desires will dictate how much food you ultimately store. As mentioned above, you will need to ease into. Don't ever stop prepping once you reach your goal of 30 days or whatever you have decided upon. It is something that is always at the forefront of your daily life. If you come across a sale that has tuna fish at .50 cents a can, by all means by 20 if you have the money. If you already have a healthy stockpile of tuna in your food stores, it doesn't matter. The more food, the better.

Food stores are not about providing enough food for the family to eat until they are full. It is about providing enough food to keep the family going strong. It is more about the calories than the actual amounts. Don't get too hung up on calorie count and try to get by with the bare minimum. There is a rule in survival prep—You can never have too much food!

Here are some facts about the amount of calories you need to survive.

*Count on an average of 2500 calories per person

*You will burn more calories in a survival situation as you chop wood, hunt, carry water and garden

*Young men will need upwards of 4000 calories to maintain their strength

*Women need fewer calories—approximately 2,200

*Children will need about 1,400 calories a day

*While you can technically go 3 weeks without eating, you will become weak, lethargic and lose muscle mass within days of not eating

Using the assumption that you want to store about 2,500 calories a day per person, use the following formula for each member of the family over the age of about 13.

2,500 x number of people in home x number of days=the amount of food.

You will need to pay attention to the labels on the food you are storing. For example, a freeze-dried meal of chili provides 400 calories per serving.

There are 16 servings in a can. 16 x 400=6,400 calories in a single can.

6,400 calories divided by 2,500 calories per person=2.5 days of food for a single person.

This will give you an idea of the amount of food we are talking about when talking about storing for a month. Of course these are just examples and many of the freeze-dried foods will have higher calorie content. This is meant to give you a real idea about the amount of food it takes to keep a family of 4 alive for a month.

Many people get into a false sense of security when they start buying those cans of freeze dried meals. It looks like a lot when it is sitting on your shelf. You figure a shelf filled with 30 gallons of freeze-dried food is going to last your family months—it won't. If you were to stock only those gallons of food, you would need about 15 per person to last a month.

Ideally, you will want to stock a variety of freeze-dried foods, canned foods, grains and beans. This will give you the freedom to change up your diet and make balanced, typical meals. Although that might sound trivial when talking about a survival situation, maintaining a sense of normalcy is extremely important to your mindset. Your kids will appreciate sitting down to a normal meal of potatoes, spaghetti and a slice of bread. All of which are possible with a well-stocked food storage.

These are some key items you will want to include in your food storage.

Meats
- Tuna
- Spam
- Chicken
- Sardines
- Jerky
- Textured vegetable protein

Grains
- Flour

- Whole wheat
- Oats
- Cornmeal
- Rice

Vegetables

- Variety of dehydrated vegetables
- Canned veggies
- Freeze-dried vegetables
- Dehydrated potatoes sliced, shredded
- Instant potatoes

Fruits

- Dehydrated fruits
- Canned fruits
- Fruit leathers

Dried beans

- Pinto
- Kidney
- Navy
- Great northern

Dairy

- Powdered milk—best for cooking
- Instant milk—best for drinking
- Powdered butter
- Powdered cheese

Pasta

- Spaghetti noodles
- Macaroni noodles
- Egg noodles

Condiments

- Salt
- Sugar
- Honey
- Variety of spices i.e. onion powder, garlic salt, oregano, cilantro
- Bouillon for soups

Luxury Goods

- Chocolate
- Chocolate powder
- Coffee
- Alcohol

Renewable Food Sources

If you live in a rural area, it makes sense to raise your own animals for the purpose of survival. A renewable food source like chickens, pigs and even cows are one way you can ensure your family always has food to eat. Chickens are prolific breeders as are pigs and rabbits. Cows are a little tougher to manage and do not reproduce s often. Goats are a better option and can provide milk.

Along with raising animals with the purpose of using them as a food source, you will also want to experiment with gardening. Not everybody can be a natural green thumb. You will want to get the hang of it before you need it to survive. Creating a garden space now will give the soil time to become fertile and more pliable to your attempt to grow food.

Water

Water is by far the biggest space hog in your food storage plan. It is bulky and there is really not much you can do about it. You need to store 1 gallon of water for each person in the house per day. 4 people in the home multiplied by 30 days equates to 120 gallons of water. That is just for drinking. That isn't factoring in cleaning or bathing. Don't panic yet. We are going to discuss some ways you can store enough water for your family. On a side note, water is an absolute necessity. It is more important than food. You can't just hope it will rain enough to keep your family watered.

If you have a well, purchase a hand pump so you can continue to pump fresh water. You can store a little water and pump the rest as needed. If you live near a body of water, you can also rely on it to supply your family with the water it needs to survive. Although it may not sound possible, that old fish pond down the road is perfectly suitable for supplying your family with water. If you are going to be hauling water, make sure to do it when it is safe. Use the buddy system whenever possible. If you are not sure about the water in your area, buy a map and use a compass to create a circle with a 5-mile radius around your home. Walking 5 miles is not a lot of fun, but it can be done. Having a wagon or cart is always a good idea if you are planning to haul water.

All water is considered dirty, unless it is coming from a well and you are not dealing with some kind of biological warfare that contaminated your water. You will need to clean all water before drinking it. You will need to store some kind of water purification system in your bug in supplies. Tablets, water filters and water purification straws are all options. Boiling the water is also a possibility if you have a barbecue or camp stove available. One of the benefits of bugging in is the fact you will have your entire kitchen at your disposal.

A useful tip about boiling water for drinking: the second the water comes to a boil it is safe! There is no need to waste water by boiling it for 5 to 10 minutes. This causes steam and evaporation and your precious water is lost! Boiling the water for a certain amount of time is a myth. The very second the water reaches boiling temperature, the pathogens are effectively killed.

Cisterns

You can plan ahead by storing a large amount of water in large vessels often referred to as cisterns. You will need some space on your property to place the cistern. They are available in a variety of sizes with some as small as 50 gallons with large ones big enough to hold 1000 gallons. These are often used on farms and places where water is scarce. There are a couple of different options you can use to place the cistern. Bury it slightly uphill from the house to take advantage of gravity or place it in the backyard or if possible, on a hill. A pipe will feed water into the house using gravity. You could also use a hand pump to pump the water out of the vessel. It is a wise idea to have a rain catchment system that will feed the cistern. Rain water is generally considered safe to drink, but if you are dealing with nuclear fallout or biological warfare, it would need to be cleaned. To be safe, boil all water before using.

Pools and Hot Tubs

Your backyard pool or your neighbor's backyard pool if they have bugged out is an excellent source of water. An average in ground pool can hold around 17,000 gallons of water. That is certainly enough to last you a while. It will be chlorinated, but the water still needs to be cleaned before drinking. A benefit to using a pool is the open top will allow it to catch rainwater. An in ground pool is not your only option. Even the kids' kiddie pool will hold water. If it is full, you have a few gallons. Leave it uncovered to catch rainwater. If you have a hot tub on the back patio, you have about 300 gallons of water at your disposal.

Rain Barrels

These are an affordable way to store 50 gallons of water. Set your rain barrels outside at the corner of your home's roof to take advantage of the runoff from a rain storm. You will be amazed at how fast these barrels fill up after a single storm. You will want to cover the top with a screen to try and keep out the majority of the debris that will run off the roof of the house and into the barrel. Keep several barrels on hand. When one barrel gets full, quickly exchange it with a new one to save every drop of water possible.

You can buy ready-made rain barrels at your local hardware store for anywhere from $50 to $100 or you can make your own for under $10. Check with restaurants and container stores and ask to buy their 50-gallon food-grade barrels. NEVER buy a barrel that has previously held chemicals. Many places will give away these barrels or leave them outside for trash pickup. One man's trash is most definitely another man's treasure! Buy a spout at your local hardware store. Drill a small hole for the spout towards the bottom of the barrel and seal it with silicon. It is an easy project that could end up saving your family's life one day.

Bottled Water

Hundreds of bottles of water are often what preppers think of when it comes to planning their emergency bugging in supplies. Bottled water is certainly convenient, quick and easy, but it is also very expensive when you consider how many gallons you need per day. Not to mention, the amount of storage space it takes is pretty substantial.

You can buy the 5-gallon water bottles to be a little more cost effective. However, these still take up a lot of space. Ideally, you want to have a supply of bottled water, along with one of the above sources to replenish the water when it is gone.

If you are planning on bottling your own water to save money, this is a possibility, but there are a few things you need to know. Do NOT use old milk jugs to store your water. This is a messy disaster waiting to happen. The jugs are made of a thin plastic that will break down over time and not a long time. It could be as little as six months before your pantry is flooded by a milk jug cracking and leaking water everywhere.

These are some containers you can use to store water long term.

- 2-liter pop bottles
- Juice bottles
- Water bottles
- 5-gallon buckets with lids
- Store bought water vessels

Before you can put your water on the shelf in your emergency food storage, it needs to be treated if you are bottling it yourself. Most people will use bleach to treat the water. While this is effective and will keep the water clean and safe to drink without further treating, it will only keep the water safe to drink for up to six months. However, and this is a big one, if you are using water from your tap and your water is already treated (which most public water is) you do not technically need to add bleach before storing. This is one of those topics of debate among preppers. It is personal preference, but many decide to err on the side of caution because you just never know—unless you have tested your tap water to check the chlorine content.

You will need to add a drop of bleach to a gallon of water and about 5 to 10 drops to large 5-gallon containers. Bleach is safe to add to your water in these minute levels. It will keep bacteria and mold growth down as your water sits on a shelf. If you are going with treated water, date the containers so you can ensure they are always fresh and ready to go. If you have fallen behind on your rotation duties and a disaster happens, you can still use the water you have stored if it is out of date. You will simply need to boil it or use water purification tablets before drinking.

When you first open a bottle of water you have stored with bleach, be prepared to smell chlorine. Let the water sit in a bowl or in the bottle with the lid off for about 30 minutes to let it freshen up. Swirl the water to help air get to the water.

How to Store Your Dry Food

If you are storing dried food like beans, rice and other grains, you need to store it properly in order to keep it fresh and free of pests. Buying in bulk is often the best way to go when purchasing dry goods. They are typically sold in plastic bags. You don't want to store them like that if at all possible. It is better to store beans, rice and grains in 5-gallon food-grade buckets with snapping lids. This will help keep out rodents that will chew right through those plastic bags. You can help prevent other pests from destroying your food stores by adding a few bay leaves to the bottom of the bucket before adding your food.

Another option is to store food in Mylar bags. The bags are vacuum sealed and can be used repeatedly. They keep food fresh for years and when stored inside a plastic bucket, you can keep out unwanted pests as well. If you are storing pastas or flour products, you will want to put the items in the freezer for a week or so before putting it in your food storage. This will kill all the weevil eggs that are in these products and yes, they are a real thing. Leave flour sitting in a warm, dry area for a few weeks and then take a look. You are likely to find tiny little bugs crawling through it.

If you have purchased freeze-dried food, you have probably seen those fantastic shelf life dates on the can. Many boast the product in the can will last for up to 25 years when stored properly. Key words there are stored properly. Your food storage, especially in the aftermath of a major disaster, isn't going to exactly be ideal. To get those kinds of shelf lives, they are referring to the foods being stored in a cool, dry, dark area at a perfect 60 to 70 degrees and the cans are unopened. Now, if you have that place in your home today, by all means use it. That is the perfect storage place. If you don't have that place, than do your best to store your food in a pantry that is not in direct sunlight, is dry and will not reach temperatures above 80.

If you have the means and the space on your property, a root cellar is an excellent storage place for some of your fresh food items. Because you never know when disaster strikes, you will always want to keep a fresh crop of potatoes, apples, carrots and onions in your root cellar. Fresh fruit and veggies in survival situation are akin to manna from heaven. You can store these foods up to a year in a root cellar by following recommended tips and guidelines. You can also store canned foods in your root cellar. Just make sure you are always rotating your food to avoid it spoiling and going to waste.

Once you open one of those cans of freeze dried foods, you have about 30 days to eat it before it becomes stale. If you have a family of four, you can easily use through a can before it becomes stale. The cans come with lids that you will want to use to keep pests out in a survival situation. Remember, cockroaches can survive pretty much anything—including a nuclear bomb. Cockroaches, mice and other pests are going to be hungry too and your food supply is going to look mighty tasty.

You can still eat food that is past its "use by" date in most cases. It may not taste quite as good, but it is still edible if not a little crunchier than usual. The best if use by is simply a guideline and does not mean you have to toss everything out. In many cases, canned foods do not have use by dates on the can or label. You will need to use your best judgment about the condition of the food.

ALWAYS check your canned food before opening and eating. Botulism is a real possibility if cans have not been stored in optimum conditions. Botulism is fatal. Home-canned foods are especially susceptible to botulism and need to be carefully inspected as well. The following are a few signs that a can of food is not safe to eat—not even a little bit!

- Rust around the edges of the can
- Dented cans need to be carefully examined to determine if there is even the slightest perforation in the can
- Bulging cans—the lids are pushing up and out
- Leaking from a can
- Food inside is molded
- Liquid in the can is abnormally cloudy
- A foul order indicating spoilage

Medical Supplies

Bugging in allows you to stock a lot more medical supplies than bugging out. Although you probably don't plan on any major medical emergencies, you are going to be doing things you may not normally do in order to survive. Accidents are inevitable. You need to be prepared to treat a wound to prevent an infection from setting in. A small cut on your finger may not be a big deal today, but in a survival situation, it could mean life or death. You have the freedom to stock a little or a lot, but if you have the means; always go on the high side. All of your preps could one day be used as bartering tools.

- Boxes of band-aids
- Several rolls of gauze
- Medical tape
- Boxes of gauze pads in varying sizes
- ACE bandage
- Bottle of pain relievers

- Latex gloves
- Cold relief medicines
- Anti-nausea meds
- Anti-diarrhea meds
- Triple biotic ointment
- Rubbing alcohol
- Peroxide
- Burn cream
- Antihistamine—Benadryl
- Antacids
- Tweezers
- Emergency tooth filling kit
- Eye drops
- Calamine lotion
- Hand sanitizer
- Extra prescription meds if you can manage to keep an extra supply

If you are familiar with homeopathic meds, you will want to stock up on these items as well. If you have never experimented with natural medicine, it is a good idea to brush up on it. You never know how long a survival situation may extend and when over-the-counter and prescription medicines will be available once again. You need to have a backup plan.

Self-Defense and Security

This is a topic of debate for many. It is a personal decision each person needs to make. Having a gun to defend yourself and your family makes sense, but not everybody is okay with the idea of actually shooting another human. It is a legitimate argument. If you do choose to have a gun or several guns, you need to have ammunition. That is another area that can prove problematic. Gun owners who are preparing to rely on their weapons in a survival situation will need to make sure ammunition is stored in a sealed, climate controlled safe or ammunition can. Guns should be kept cleaned and in top working condition as well.

Pepper spray, knives and Tasers are all options as well, but hand-to-hand combat should be avoided at all costs. There is a strong possibility you will be injured in some way, even if you are the victor. Learning self-defense is a good idea and can help you ensure a victory if you are forced to defend yourself or your home.

The government recommends you keep a roll of sturdy plastic on hand to cover windows and doors in the event of a biological attack. You will likely have towels on hand to place under the doors as well. Vents will also need to be covered.

Miscellaneous Gear

If you are bugging in, you have the freedom to really load up on pretty much anything you need should you be forced to survive off what you have in the home. While food and water are typically the top two priorities, there are some other things you will need to survive a long period of time. It could take years for the world to recover from a major event. That means that although people will start to pick up the pieces of their lives and rebuild, there is still going to be a time period when grocery stores shelves are not stocked. Basic necessities are going to be in short supply, but in high demand.

If you have the room, you will want to start storing the following items as well.

- Toilet paper
- Feminine hygiene products
- Soap
- Heirloom seeds—these will produce fruits and vegetables with seeds that can be replanted to continue growing food.
- Hammer and nails—you never know when you need to make repairs
- Axe—chopping wood for heat will be a strong possibility
- Gardening tools i.e. shovel, rake, hoe—you are your own grocery store
- Hunting and fishing gear—see above
- Personal hygiene i.e. toothpaste, deodorant, shampoo, chapstick
- Face masks in case of pandemic or biological warfare. You also need to be prepared for the stench of death and decay.
- Heat source—wood stove, propane or kerosene heaters (have a supply of propane and kerosene on hand)

- Heavy duty garbage bags—there will not be garbage men and you need to keep your home clean to avoid bacteria and disease
- Entertainment—books, board games, crossword puzzles, cards are all things you can toss into your storage area that will help pass the time. You are probably going to be very surprised how much time is on your hand when you don't have computers, cell phones, gaming systems and television.
- Bleach—for cleaning your home and purifying your water. However, bleach does weaken over time. You can typically expect a gallon of bleach to last about a year.

Securing Your Home and Supplies

Creating an adequate food storage plan is extremely time-consuming and labor intensive. It can also be a huge investment of the family's funds. You need to protect it with everything you have. It is what is going to keep you alive when things are tough. If you are going to be bugging in, you need to make sure your supplies are secure and not susceptible to the looters and other folks who did not prepare. As was mentioned earlier, people are going to come looking. Many preppers are very secretive about what they have even among fellow preppers who they deem friends. This is because you just never know! People turn on each other when it comes down to a life and death situation. Put yourself in somebody else's shoes. If your child were starving, wouldn't you be willing to do almost anything to feed him or her?

It may sound a little cliché, but one of the first rules of prepping is not to talk about what you have. You can certainly talk with others about what they may want to store and what you think would be a really good idea to store, but you don't want to say, "I have a 12-month supply of food and water in my basement." Keep it to yourself! Educate your children as well. They don't need to tell all their friends about what they have in their basement. Kids talk and if they are starving after a catastrophe, they are going to tell others about what so and so told them a while ago. You would have a mob at your door and your family's safety would be in serious jeopardy.

Securing your supplies can be as simple as keeping them out of sight or as intricate as hiding them in a panic room or other secret space in your home. This is sometimes where people get the wrong idea about preppers. Preppers are often called weird or crazy for going to great lengths to hide their supplies. But, when you think of how much time and money is involved in creating a year's supply of food, it isn't all that crazy. People hide their valuables in wall safes and other nooks and crannies all the time. It is normal to want to protect things of value and when there are no grocery stores, government aid or fast food restaurants, food is going to be more valuable than precious jewels.

While a state-of-the art panic room is a dream many preppers have, it is just not feasible for most due to the cost. Bunkers are also a luxury that many preppers dream about, but again, it isn't always possible, especially for suburban preppers.

It is best to secure your home to keep out those who will try and take what you have. We will discuss securing your supplies next. A simple lock on a front door is not going to keep out the baddies. Windows and sliding glass doors are an open invitation. There are some preppers who have invested in bullet-proof glass for sliding glass doors. This is a great idea, but again, pretty costly. Many will go about putting shatter-proof glass in place of glass windows on the bottom floor of their houses. This is a common practice for people who are worried about burglaries. However, you need to consider the risks of living in a house that would impede escape if ever there were a fire.

Another way to secure your home's windows is by keeping some plywood on hand. When disaster strikes, or just before if you know it is coming, nail the wood over the windows to keep intruders from breaking the glass. If it is a storm system you are preparing to whether, this can keep your home intact as well and keep you safe from breaking glass.

Invest in sturdy door locks or create a bar system that makes it difficult to kick in a door. These can be found online or at some home improvement stores. Investing in solid metal doors is a worthy investment. DO NOT put pet doors in your front or back doors! This is an invitation for thieves in any situation. Bars on windows are an option, but you have to remember you are going to be living in your house when things are "normal." Bars on the window are often a signal that you have something of value inside and you may be targeted by thieves before disaster ever strikes.

Many experts agree that protecting your home's perimeter is the best way to go. It is likely the power will be out, but you can buy motion detector lights that are solar powered. This will at least give you advanced warning that somebody is headed your way. Cameras or a security system are great, but will only work if you have power. If you are savvy enough to hook your security system up to a car battery, that is always an option or maybe you have already invested in solar power.

You can still hide your food supply throughout your home or apartment. A single pantry may seem like a good place to store all your food and it is, but it is also the first place a looter is going to look. There are several other places in your home you could hide your food, water and other emergency supplies that will not attract the attention of unwanted visitors. Basically, you want to follow some of the guidelines mentioned in the hiding of a bug out bag. There are a few more places you can store food and other emergency supplies, including weapons. Check out some of these ideas and see if you can make them work for you.

- Behind the couch. You can create a behind-the-couch table that will successfully hide a great deal of food. There are can organizers that are as wide as the height of a can of food. You could stack several on top of each other and place between the wall and couch. Put a piece of wood over the top of the can holder and add a few pretty candles. It will look like a piece of furniture.

- Create a false bottom in your closets. Line up canned foods along the bottom of the closet. Put a piece of wood over the canned foods and dump your shoes, bags and what not on top. Anybody who pulls the closet open will see the typical contents.

- Your child's toy box is another great place to stash supplies. Create a false bottom that the kids cannot remove. Most kids won't bother trying to remove the bottom of a toy box anyways. Once they reach the bottom, they move on.

- You could certainly utilize the space under your bed, but realize many burglars and looters will look there first. However, use dark colored totes to stash your supplies in. Label the totes "winter clothes" or something along those lines. Thieves who are in a hurry may not take the time to rifle through the tote.

- Fill your attic space with totes and boxes of "grandma's things" and "holiday decorations," but in reality, your supplies would be mingled among the boxes of what would be perceived as junk.

- A hook on the back of your bedroom door that holds your bathrobe could double as a place to hide a weapon or a first aid kit. Hang the item on the hook and throw a dingy bathrobe over the top. Thieves won't look twice. Be careful not to hang anything too heavy as this may alert the thief to your hiding spot.

Teaching the Whole Family the Bug In Plan

If bugging in is your goal, you need to make sure the whole family is on board. You need to have a plan for each family member to follow in the event of an emergency. It is almost impossible to predict when or where disaster will strike. There is a good chance you and your family will not be home when it all hits the fan. If you are planning to bug in, you need to make sure you have a plan to get everybody home. Every family will have a different plan. However, every member of the household will have an ultimate goal of making it home. Check out the following example.

*You and your spouse both work. The spouse works outside of town, while you work in town. Your oldest child attends high school, which is within a block or two of your youngest child's elementary school. Plan A—you as the in-town spouse will figure out a way to drive, walk or bicycle to the kids' school. Oldest student will have already rounded up youngest sibling and will be waiting across the street from the school for in-town spouse to escort home. Out of town spouse goes directly home.

*Plan B-Oldest student finds younger sibling and makes the trek home along a designated, pre-planned route. In town spouse follows same route if possible to pick up the kids.

In the immediate hours and days following a disaster, your family may opt to hole up in the basement, a safe room or a designated area in the house. Typically, your best bet is below ground. If you have a basement, you will likely want to hide there until things have settled down a bit. You need each member of the family to know where they are supposed to be when they hear the emergency sirens outside or mom and dad have said, "This is it!" You, as the adult, will not have time to collect children, gather any additional supplies, lock up and get to the designated area. If you have several children, have an older one responsible for getting a younger one to the right place.

Plan ahead who is going to lock the front door, who is going to shut off the main gas to the home and who is going to get the pets into the home. Run drills often to make sure everybody knows exactly what they are supposed to do in an emergency. Teach your children the importance of dropping everything and getting into the safe room. You absolutely want everybody together so you can take a head count. If your home is already secured and you are planning on bugging in without holing up in a particular area, you still need a meeting point so you can account for every member of the household. This is also the time you will want to go through the checklist of things that needed to happen to ensure your bugging in is going to be a safe place for the family.

Bugging In Checklist
- Shut off all utilities just in case—water, gas, electric
- Lock doors and windows—put sticks in windows to prevent them from being opened
- Use wood to cover windows if possible from the inside so outsiders are not aware somebody took the time to secure the

home. The curtains or blinds will look normal hanging in the window.

- Make the toilet (see section below)
- Cover windows with blackout curtains or blankets if you don't have wood (you don't want others to know you are in the house)
- Grab flashlights and candles but only use when necessary to avoid detection
- Discuss what everybody will need to do for the next 24 hours
- Relax and keep everybody calm, sing songs, pray, read stories or do whatever helps your family relax.

Bug In Toilet

It isn't something anybody likes to talk about, but no matter what is happening in the world, humans still have to poop and pee. When you bug in, you are likely going to be in your home without a working toilet. If you live in the country and have a septic tank, you are still going to have to flush the toilet without power. This is a waste of water, but if water isn't a problem, consider yourself one of the fortunate ones. Because you are going to be in your home, you can't allow it to become filthy. Human waste harbors a host of bacteria and viruses that could make you and your family extremely ill. Cleanliness is extra important when you are bugging in.

1-Have a 5-gallon bucket ready
2-Have a roll of heavy-duty garbage bags

3-Line the bucket with garbage bag—to be extra careful, double line the bucket.

4-Use the bucket as a toilet and dump as needed.

5-When toilet isn't in use, cover with a lid to cut down on the smell.

If you are on a large piece of land and can safely go outside to use the toilet, do so. You can dig a hole in the ground, cut out the bottom of a bucket and place it over the hole to use as a toilet. Cover the hole every few days to cut down on smell. Place a rock or piece of wood over the area to keep animals from digging it up.

Pets—Do You Keep Them or Abandon Them?

Your family's pets are likely one of the family. You love them dearly and couldn't imagine leaving them outside as you bug in or leaving them behind if you bug out. That is a sentiment many pet owners share, but you must consider your family's needs first. Could you split the last can of beans with your pet? It isn't really fair to bring your pet along for the ride only to let it starve when food runs low. Sanitation could also be an issue if you are bugging in. If it is a cat, a litter box is adequate. If you have dogs, you are going to have to pay close attention to their bathroom needs. You will need to make sure you can open a door to let the pet out to do their business without calling attention to the fact you are holed up in your home. It is absolutely not sanitary to let the animals do their business in the place you will be eating and sleeping.

On the flip side of the argument, having what may be your best friend or your child's best friend by your side when things are scary is a huge comfort. This is true of bugging in or bugging out. Being able to pet your animal is comforting. Your children will take great pleasure in having a companion with them that is from their life before things got ugly.

There is also the possibility your pet could be an additional layer of security. You don't have to have an attack dog, but a dog will defend its owners and property instinctively. This is a handy tool to have along with you when you are trekking to a body of water to retrieve water for your house. If you have bugged out, a dog is a hyper-sensitive alert system. Dogs can hear and smell intruders and predators long before a human ever could. This is like an early warning system for you. It gives you time to hide or prepare for intruders.

If your dog has been trained to hunt, this is another very good reason to bring it along. There is a strong possibility you will need to return to the old ways of hunting and gathering. Having a dog along can make the job much easier and more effective. If you have bugged out and the temperatures are freezing, snuggling with your pet is an excellent way to maintain your core body temperature.

Once you have weighed all the pros and cons of keeping your pet or several pets with you, it is time to make a decision. You need to make the decision before an emergency arises. It is almost impossible to make a logical decision when your pet is yapping to come along with you when you bug out. It is an emotional decision that you want to take the time to evaluate carefully before you are forced to do so.

If you do plan on keeping the pets with you when you bug out or bug in, you need to expand your preps to include dog food. You will also need to factor in the additional water needed to support the animals.

Deciding to Bug In or Bug Out

This is one of the toughest decisions you will have to make. It is best to decide before an event happens. You want to use logic to make such a life-changing choice—not emotion. It is natural you would want to hunker down in your home, where all of your things are and where you feel most comfortable. Bugging in gives you the chance to really stockpile everything you need to survive in the aftermath of a devastating storm, an economic collapse or whatever it is that has befallen you.

There is always a lot of talk about bugging out, but that may not be what is right for you and your family. It does seem the prepping world gets a little bug out happy. People are always talking about the bug out bags and how to survive off the land. While that is all very important, why do that if you don't have to? Sleeping outside when it is snowing and the temperature is hovering around 20 degrees and you have nothing more than a space blanket to keep you warm isn't exactly ideal. Don't be too quick to plan on bugging out. It is exciting when you sit in your comfortable chair drinking your hot coffee and reading about it, but actually doing it is an entirely different ball game. Roughing it isn't always that fun once the novelty wears off. If you absolutely must leave your home, fine, but don't just assume you have to bug out when disaster strikes.

There are several factors that will need to be considered before making a decision. Do not wait to make such an important decision. Talk with your family members and get their input. If you know anybody who you would consider an experienced survivalist, get their opinion as well. Make a list of pros and cons. Brainstorm the various scenarios and make the decision to bug out if there is a terrorist attack but bug in if there is a pandemic or whatever the case may be. This preplanning will make things go much smoother when it is time to take action.

Even if you reach a decision to bug in or to bug out, you need to be prepared to do the opposite, just in case. If you have decided you are going to bug out, there is a chance it will not be safe for you to leave your home if the weather is bad or there are gunmen out there waiting to take you out. On the flipside, if you have decided to bug in and a major storm strikes and turns your home to rubble, you need to bug out. Always have a backup. Part of the prepping mentality is to prep for whatever disaster may strike. You are storing food, water and medical supplies because there is a chance things could go very bad and you are going to be forced to survive on your preps. There are no certainties in a chaotic world. You have only yourself and your closest friends and family members to count on.

Where You Live Matters

Your decision to bug in or bug out is going to weigh heavily on where you live. If you live in a rural area on a nice piece of land and the nearest neighbors are a ½ mile away, bugging in is completely doable and probably warranted. If you live in an apartment in the city, bugging out may be a better option. As a general rule of thumb, preppers will want to get out of Dodge so to speak when things are in chaos. More people, means more problems, like people trying to take what you have. Large cities become targets for attacks if it is a war or act of terror you are up against.

One of the first rules of survival is finding shelter. If your home no longer provides you with adequate shelter from the elements it is time to go. Maybe it was damaged by a natural disaster or the foundation has been compromised by an explosion. If the shelter isn't safe, it is absolutely crucial to bug out.

Another factor may be the location of your home. Floods are often a side effect of certain natural disasters. Homes that are too close to a body of water and are at risk of being flooded should be evacuated. Apartments in high rises are often targets for bombs if we are under a terror attack or there is civil unrest. Earthquakes may make the structure unsafe.

You can determine what kind of natural disasters your home is most likely to experience by checking some history. Answer the following questions to help you identify risks that could put a bug in plan in danger.

- Do you live in tornado alley?

- Do you live along a fault line?
- Do you live high up in the mountains where snowfall is excessive?
- Are you surrounded by desert?
- Do you live near a nuclear power plant?

These are all questions that will help you identify any potential dangers that could make your home a disaster waiting to happen. No matter how much you love your home and you love the things in your home, if it is in danger of being destroyed with you in it, you have to leave it all behind.

Do You Have Somewhere to Go

Probably one of the biggest factors in determining whether or not you bug out is if you have anywhere to go! Do you bug out and plan on living off the land until things settle down (which could be months or years) or do you hunker down where you at least have a roof over your head? Really prepared people will have a location to bug out too. The second location is where they will hunker down and ride out whatever disaster has shaken things up.

The second location will likely be a smaller home located in a rural area. A cabin in the woods, a bunker underground or a ranch house that looks like it has been abandoned all make excellent destinations. These second homes can be stocked with everything you need to survive. However, and this is a big one, can you get there?

- If you don't have a car, can you and your family walk to the second location?
- If you have a car, do you have gas to get there?
- Will the route to your destination be closed if there is a major disaster? Bridge crossings are not always reliable.
- Is your route through the heart of the city?
- Do you need 4WD to reach the location?

If you are planning to bug out to another location, it is important you plot out a Plan A, Plan B and if all else fails, a Plan C route. If you are leaving the city, expect there to be a LOT of traffic. Highways may be clogged and you could end up being stuck in a horrible traffic jam. A backup plan may not be the quickest route and may involve a series of back roads, but they are less likely to be jammed up. Finally, a plan when all else fails should be in place. This may mean walking, biking or taking a boat to your secondary location.

Closing Thoughts

Preparing to survive an event that will turn the world as we know it upside down isn't easy. There are a lot of different bases to cover. We have it pretty easy right now. When we need something, we run to the store and buy it, borrow it from a friend or ask our family to help us get it. We have become accustomed to relying on various charity organizations and the government to help those who have been devastated by a natural disaster or some other horrific event. If we see something illegal, we call the police and they take care of the bad guy. If we get a broken bone or our child has a high fever, we go to the doctor.

Life isn't so bad when you list out all those luxuries we have and they truly are luxuries. When all of that is taken away, it is just you and those you can call true friends. There won't be anybody to come to your rescue. Taking the time to plan what you need today can ultimately save your life down the road and the lives of your loved ones.

Some people attach the words paranoid or crazy to the prepping movement. Those people assume nothing bad will ever happen. Some of those same people will also say that if something terrible were to happen, it is best to die with the rest of the community. A prepper will say *that* is what is crazy. Why give up when there is always a chance? If there is a chance you could keep your child alive and even thriving in a new world, it sounds crazy *not* to try and do it.

It is your life and you must do what you feel is right for you and your family. Don't worry about those who call you crazy and a freak. It is probably best if you don't really advertise you are one of those who is preparing to survive. There will be some of those naysayers who do survive and they will remember their crazy neighbor or co-worker and come calling.

The most important thing is to have a plan. Any plan. If you have some sort of plan, you will be better prepared than 99% of the population. And that advantage could very well be the thing that saves you and your family. So start prepping, start early, and stick with it!

*****

If you've enjoyed this book, **please** consider leaving a review and letting others know what you thought!

Sign up for Robert's Mailing List to be notified of **New Releases** and **Special Sales**: http://eepurl.com/zvm11

No Spam – he promises!

*****

Other Books by Robert Paine:
The Ultimate Prepper Collection: Survival Guides For Every Situation
Prepper's Pantry: A Survival Food Guide
The Survivalist Cookbook - Recipes for Preppers
Prepping 101: A Beginner's Survival Guide
The Dead Road: The Complete Collection